It's Campmeeting Time ...IN THE CHOIR LOFT

EASY TO PREPARE, FUN TO SING
Arranged by MOSIE LISTER

Lillenas PUBLISHING COMPANY

KANSAS CITY, MO 64141

Singin' Camp Meetin' Style

Arr. by Mosie Lister

*"Singin' Camp Meetin' Style" (Mosie Lister)

I like that sing-in', _____ camp meet-in' style. _____ It makes you

hap-py, it makes you smile. For you'll love your fel-low man, And the

CD: 2

Choir unison

feel-in's might-y grand When you're sing-in' camp meet-in' style. 1. I re-

C   G   Em   Cm6/Eb   G/D   N.C.   D7   G

(2nd time: ladies only)

call camp meet-in' days   And those   grand old songs of praise.   I   re-
hear the preach-er   now   Preach-in'   'bout the heav'n-ly pow'r   As   the
voic-es   in ac-cord   Sing-ing   prais-es   to   the Lord.   You   could

G   C

2nd time: men only

mem-ber   tho' but a child.____   'Twas a might-y joy-ful sound When the
sin-ners   came down the aisle.____   As the   con-gre-ga-tion sang, How "Old-
hear them   more than a   mile.____   There were tear drops in their eyes,   But their

C/G   G   D   Am7   D   G

4

CD: 3

**"Give Me That Old-time Religion" (Anon., arr. by Mosie Lister)*

Ladies unison *Div.*

love your fel - low man, And the feel - in's might - y grand When you're

sing - in' _____ camp meet - in' style, When you're

sing-in' _____ camp meet - in' style. _____

These Are They

W. J. G. and G. G.

WILLIAM J. and GLORIA GAITHER
Arr. by Mosie Lister

blood   of   the   Lamb.   They're re -

deemed   by   the   blood   of   the   Lamb,   of   the

Lamb.

One of His Own

M. L.

MOSIE LISTER

stands by me   And claims me   as_____ one of His own.   One of His
hand in mine,   Con - tent to

own_____ is all I   want to be.   Where He may   lead,_____ I'll fol-low

on.   For this I   know:_____ what-ev-er comes to me,   I'll al-ways

The Old Landmark

UNKNOWN

UNKNOWN
Arr. by Mosie Lister

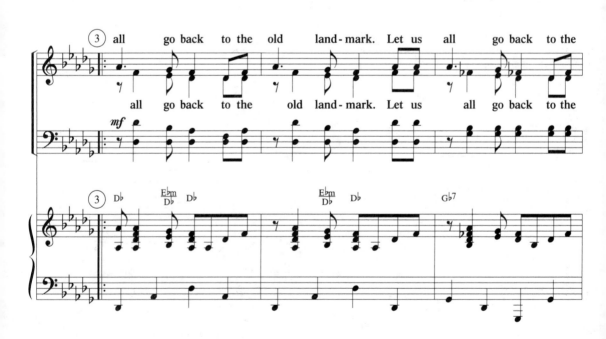

And He will

old - time way.   kneel and pray   old - time way. And He will
old - time way. Let us kneel   and pray   in the old - time way,

Db   Ebm/Db Db   Ebm/Db Db   Ebm/Db Db

18 hear us and be near us. He will feed us bread from heav - en, And we'll

hear us   near us.   feed us   heav - en,

Div.

18 Db

CD: 16   Unison

stay in the ser - vice of the Lord.   Come now, you

Unison

Db Db/F Ebm/Gb Db/Ab Ab7 Db   Db/Cb A

preach-ers, preach the Word_____ straight_ and ho - ly;

Preach it to the whole_____ con - gre - ga - tion._____ In the

might and the pow - er of_ the Spir - it, Preach it now with-out_____ hes - i -

Alleluia to the King

M. L.

MOSIE LISTER

Soon! Medley

Arr. by Mosie Lister

32

CD: 22

*"I Won't Turn Back" (Mosie Lister)

Suddenly faster, with a shuffle ♩ = 150

CD: 23

I'll keep hold-ing on. I I'll keep

hold - ing on,

hold - ing on!

The Day of Miracles

M. L.

MOSIE LISTER

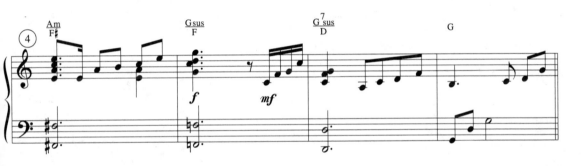

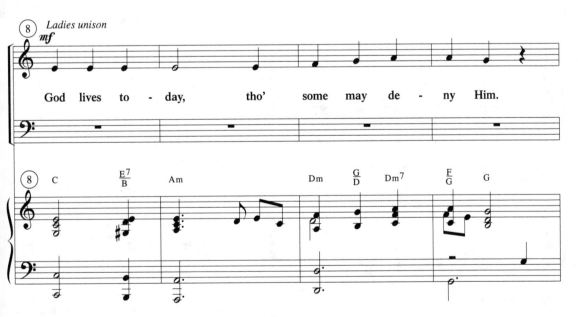

God lives to-day, tho' some may de-ny Him.

moun-tain_____ still cares for you and me, And the day of

mir-a-cles_____ is the day_____ you be-

lieve,_____ be - lieve!_____

Love Medley

Arr. by Mosie Lister

Thank God, I Am Free

J. McF.

JAMES McFALL
Arr. by Mosie Lister

gain.   Hal - le - lu - jah, I'm saved, saved,   saved by His won-der-ful

grace.   I'm so glad that I found out   He would bring me out and show me the

way.   Thank God, I am   free,   free,   free from this world of

CD: 30 *1st time*

Unison

48

Power in the Name of Jesus

G. E. A.

GLEN E. AUBREY
Arr. by Mosie Lister

13

And that name, that___ won - der - ful name so
For in Je - sus'___ name all God's pow'r is

F7 F7/A Gm/Bb D7 D+ D7 Gm

17 CD: 32 *1st time*
CD: 34 *2nd time*

2nd time to Coda ⊕

dear is___ Je - sus, Je - sus my Lord.
ours to___ con - quer each en - e -

Eb9 F/C Bb/C Am/C C7 F

21

There is pow'r in the name of Je -

Choir *mf*

Pow'r in the name,___ in the name of

mf

Bb/C C **21** F F+ F5#9 Bb

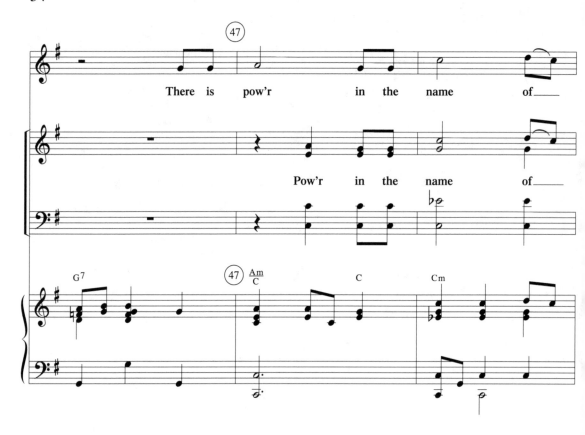

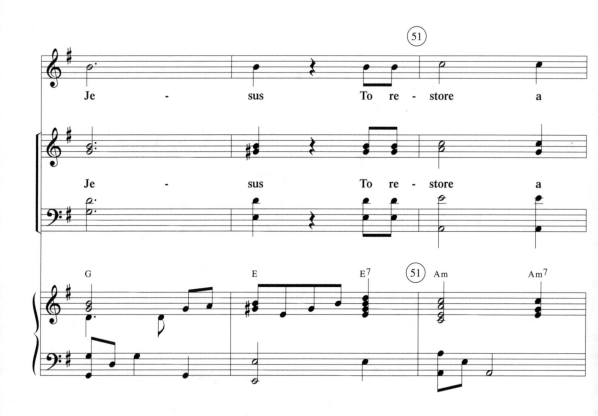

Jubilee Medley

Arr. by Mosie Lister

*"The Happy Jubilee" (Raymond Browning - Adger M. Pace)

Praise the Lord, I've been in-vit-ed to a meet-ing in the air. Ju-bi-lee! Ju-bi-lee! Ju-bi-lee! Ju-bi-lee! All the

58

60

*"When We All Get to Heaven" (Eliza Hewitt - Emily D. Wilson)

More and More

M. L.

MOSIE LISTER

day   I love Him,   oh, so much bet - ter.

Ev - 'ry day I   love   Him

more,   more and more.

At the Crossing

M. L.

MOSIE LISTER

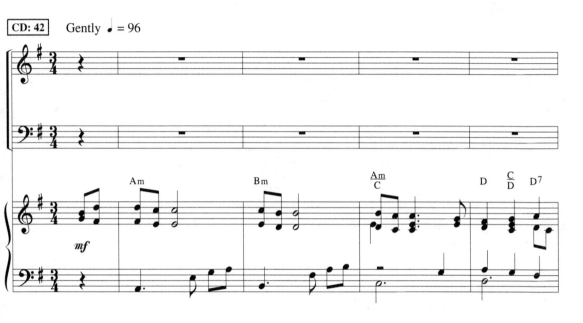

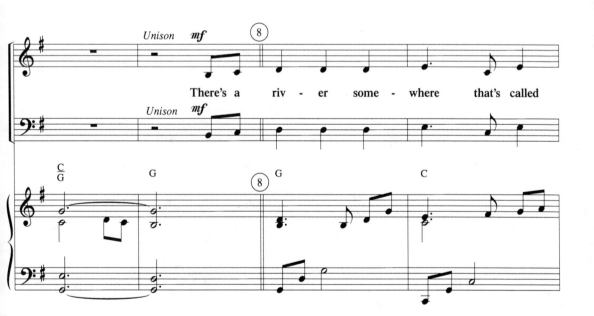

70

Surrendered, Completely Surrendered

S. R. A.

STEPHEN R. ADAMS
Arr. by Mosie Lister

My God Can Do Anything

V. E.

VEP ELLIS
Arr. by Mosie Lister

With confidence ♩ = 96

Choir unison on melody **mf**

Lyrics:
My God can do an-y-thing, an-y-thing, yes, an-y-thing. My God can do an-y-thing. My God can do an-y-thing._____ He made this earth with all its

Blessed Be the Name of the Lord

C. U.

CLINTON UTTERBACK
Arr. by Mosie Lister

I Believe in a Hill Called Mount Calvary

W. J. G., GLORIA GAITHER, and DOUG OLDHAM

WILLIAM J. GAITHER
Arr. by Mosie Lister

Lyrics:

There are things as we trav-el this earth's shift-ing sands That tran-scend all the rea-son of man;

lieve, what - ev - er the cost._____ And when

time_____ has sur - ren - dered,_____ and earth is no more, I'll still

cling to the old rug - ged cross. I be -

He's Everything to Me

M. L.

MOSIE LISTER

liv-ing in my heart, Nev-er to de-part; He's ev - 'ry-thing to___

Liv - ing in my heart, Nev - er to de-part, Ev - 'ry-thing to

me.

me.

D.S. al Coda

CD: 60

CODA

be. Now He is ev-'ry-thing to me And

God Said It, I Believe It, That Settles It

S. R. A. and GENE BRAUN

STEPHEN R. ADAMS
Arr. by Mosie Lister

100

All Your Anxiety

E. H. J.

EDWARD HENRY JOY
Arr. by Mosie Lister

I've Found a New Friend

M. L.

MOSIE LISTER

I've found a new Friend; He's such a true Friend.

He walks be - side me_____ and holds my hand.

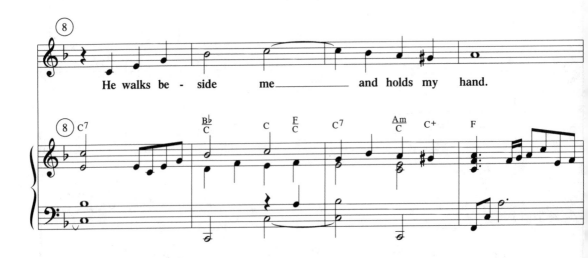

CONTENTS